Aida Noor Thoughts

I think I write I speak

Aida Noor

A career journey of finding my way

A career journey that led to self-discovery

Dedication to my mother:

I am grateful to have the best mother in the world. She was a game-changer herself and she made me believe that I can be who I want to be, she always wanted me to be the best version of myself and never stop dreaming.

Contents

Let me introduce myself.

I am a scientist, a scientist with a vision. I had a challenging journey in perusing my career. Which turned out to be a self-discovery and a self-awareness journey, where my professional development led to my personal development. I discovered that they both complement each other and that is the secret to success and achieving my goals. I wish they told me this when I was at school or even at university.

I am a Biomedical Scientist, a healthcare scientist. I had an interesting journey pursuing my career to become a qualified professional. It was not an easy journey; it was filled with challenges which eventually led to more opportunities.

I wanted to share the personal side of my career journey as not many people in my industry, the healthcare, and the scientific industry, talk about how they felt overcoming the challenges, or how they felt going through them, particularly in my industry, science, and healthcare. They only talk about it briefly and it sounds like it was short and quick. No, it is not it is a journey and a process, sometimes it can consist of several steps some are longer and some quicker.

The most important part of the journey is the person that you become and the lessons that you learn along the way.

So, I decided to document my journey so that you can benefit from my experience and not repeat my mistakes. Hopefully, it will make you realise that having a different route or path does not make you a failure, it may lead you to become a leader or even a creator in your special way. Looking back, I am aware of the person that I have become, I know what I want, and I know if I believe in myself, and I put in the work and the effort I will get what I want to achieve. So, you should think that way too, never give up on your dreams no matter how long it may take you to reach them.

Introduction.

When you are about to start your career, you will inevitably face many challenges. Every career has its challenges. The difference is the lessons that you learn from your career journey as these will shape you. My career journey was not easy it was somehow lengthy. I remember at one point I said to myself I going to share this with the world to help and inspire others.

I share some of the lessons that I have learned from my journey that I believe they can apply to any career journey, some of which may overlap but collectively in my opinion they all matter.

Becoming a qualified Biomedical Scientist in the UK was not straightforward, I took the long route, and from there my professional and the personal transformation began, so I decided to share the personal side of it.

No matter how challenging it can be, you must remind yourself that it will get done in the end, and you will get there as a winner.

I wanted to share my story so that it will hopefully inspire you and remind you that you are not alone. We have all been there, done that.

I want you to see that every challenge brings an opportunity with it. Period.

Some might disagree with this, but I guarantee you that if look at all the successful people who did it, they saw that challenges bring opportunities with them. However, you need to be able to see the opportunity to go through the challenge.

I always loved science when I was at school, so I decided to become a scientist I just wanted to make a difference for a better world with no diseases. I was not interested in becoming a doctor I just wanted a different career. However, my journey to become a qualified healthcare scientist, and to become a Biomedical Scientist was not easy for many reasons that I will explain later in this book.

I was born and bred in Abu-Dhabi the capital of UAE. I had a great childhood and I enjoyed school, then I graduated from secondary school. It was time to pursue my university studies, so I decided to move to the UK.

So, what inspired me to share my career story, to be honest, I do not want you to make the same mistakes that I have made, I want you to learn from my experience. Maybe you are feeling alone in your career journey, and you feel that you are about to give up, please don't!

I was always passionate about science.

I chose science because I loved it since I was at school, but I did not realise that my journey with science would be an interesting one. I hope my journey will help you to continue chasing your dreams and goals and never give up just because you are facing hardships.

After graduating and completing my undergraduate Biochemistry degree, I did not know what to do next. In my time we did not have career mentors it was not that popular back then, although there were career advisors and career university centres, I did not feel the need to approach them, also getting work experience was still optional and there was no pressure to get it before graduating. Life was straightforward back then or I thought it was, I was so naïve. I would recommend that you connect with career advisors and the student union of your university or college or high school, you never know who may help you or guide you in your career.

That lost feeling of what next after years of studying was the scariest, so I just went full-time on my part-time job. I then resigned to focus on my next career move, I remember I was not working for almost a year I spent it reading and learning about what I wanted to do next in science. Looking back this was my first career break experience or sometimes referred to as "Sabbatical Year" if you are reading this book, you must have heard the benefits of having a career break.

During that year I remember I went to my local hospital and met the laboratory supervisor and he explained that I needed to get my degree assessed and find a trainee position to become Biomedical Scientist. This was disheartening, as this was not emphasised when I was at university. To do a one-year work experience in a laboratory or a pharmaceutical company again was optional, so most of us thought let us finish our studies quickly and then can be free to enter the workforce.

This was the biggest mistake that I have made, getting work experience enhances your career options, I talk about this now all the time, in my writings, when I speak at panels or events, and I tell the students that I mentor. Make sure that you get some relevant work experience while you are studying.

In the UK, to become a Biomedical Scientist aka BMS, in short, you must complete an Institute Biomedical Science (IBMS) portfolio, get assessed by them and then register with the Health and Care Professional Council (HCPC). Then you become a registered Biomedical Scientist.

The IBMS is the leading professional body for scientists, support staff and students in the field of biomedical science.

The Health and Care Professions Council are an organisation which regulates health, psychological and care professionals in the United Kingdom. They set standards, hold a register, quality assure education and investigate complaints.

If you complete a sandwich year this is done while you are studying for your bachelor's degree and you become registered and apply to work as BMS, if not you will have to take a longer route, which I have taken, unfortunately!

With my undergraduate Biochemistry degree, I did not know what to do with it and towards the end, I did not enjoy it or maybe I lost the drive I do not know what happened back then.

So, cutting the story short my mum suggested that I should do my Master's, this was the best advice back then as it gets harder to do further studies once you enter the workforce, and I realised that later in life.

I chose to study Biomedical Science- Medical Microbiology, I remember I did not like that field during my previous studies, but I wanted to challenge myself. I was so scared when I got to my place for the course. it was all new to me, I remember I went to the library and got all the books that I thought will help me to study the new discipline that I chose I remember that time for two weeks I was reading the foundation material. I decided to fully dedicate myself to studying, for a full year, it was the best year of my life, and I loved every part of it.

Then I got a temporary position as a Research Scientist in a pharmaceutical company where I was incredibly happy that I got the job within a few months after graduating, and within a few weeks of my graduation ceremony.

Later that year, my next goal was to work in a hospital laboratory. I got a medical laboratory assistant position in a diagnostic company where I wanted to apply what I have learned.

It started all well I moved departments within two years from reception to microbiology, this period was valuable for me as I learned so much about diagnostic laboratories. After years of working and moving departments, I did not go anywhere in my aim to become a qualified scientist.

So, I decided to take the leap and start again in another hospital until I finally became a qualified Biomedical Scientist, which took years to achieve with many highs and lows. But many lessons were learned.

I did not give up on my dream of qualifying, I was even going from a permanent position to a temporary one, and then I got a permanent one when one was available within two months of joining.

Can professional development lead to personal development?

Knowing myself was the most important step.

Before I dive into my development journey, I want to explain how I learned that personal development is essential for achieving both personal and professional success.

Normally you hear that people go through a self-discovery to know their true purpose in life and then they choose their lives and careers. That is not always the case, well in my case. The first year of my new professional development journey has led me to discover more about myself and what I wanted in life. Then that led to more professional development, I learned that they both complement each other. Once you know who you are, you will know what you want. It might be tough at first but believe me, it does get easier. When you have a solid foundation or roots – knowing yourself- then you know what you want.

So, the first year for me was a discovery journey in every aspect in terms of the work environment, the people, the culture outside London and taking a new career path filled with life lessons from the professional development journey. After working and developing my career in the private sector I moved to work for the NHS which was the best experience for me professionally.

A new start.

I remember back at the end of that year as we were approaching the new year, I was having a random conversation with someone back then, about the new year and feeling positive about what the new year is holding for us. The pessimistic response that I got from that person was just shocking, she said "We said that last year about this year, what makes you feel that the new year will be different".

I didn't think much about it at that time, but later on, I deeply thought about it and that year was the year for me where I thought this is it, I need to do something different in my life, so while I was going through my first professional development journey, I started first personal development journey. I learned so much, and I want to share it with you because I think I need to share the personal side of this experience and how the way I think of myself has helped me to make better career decisions. This has originated from my professional-personal experience to become a qualified scientist.

1st February 2017, I remember that day very well I decided enough is enough I need to stop living an ordinary working life and waiting for the weekend. I started by applying small changes in my daily habits, my gut instinct down I felt I should start small and that will lead to bigger changes. By simply changing my daily routine, going to bed early and waking up early, this powerful change has led to other bigger changes, which I will elaborate on further in the book.

I must admit I did not know where to start this was the first time that I wanted to know myself more I must admit I was incredibly lucky. I learned that every aspect of your life will depend on that when you know yourself you know what you want in life.

I remember back then my best friend suggested a book by "The Magic of Thinking Big" by David Schwartz my life has never been the same, and I highly recommend reading it. After I read that book, I just stayed focused on myself and started discovering more about myself and my surroundings.

I started to enjoy my own company and explore more, which I never knew how important it is to explore alone. I used it before, but I did not have that curious mind of every detail or I was missing the awareness element, I enjoyed that year of rediscovering myself, my family, my friends, and the whole world around me.

I have learned a valuable lesson that knowing yourself will help you know what you want in life at whatever age or stage.

Positive thinking.

The following year I wanted to expand and the next step of my journey, is to think positive, yes it has its magic, but I never appreciated how important it is to think positive. But since I changed my mindset, my life has never been the same since. I cannot explain how I developed that, there is no secret recipe, it is a process where you gradually build that mindset.

I remember I just started to change the way I think about things in general. I stopped about the things that can go wrong and just started to think about what can go right instead. Slowly that becomes the norm. I never fear anything anymore

Think how children never think negatively they go for it because they never have any expectations. I think this is also linked to knowing yourself, once I learned about myself my strengths and weaknesses and I was aware of who I am, then I changed the way

I think of everything in my life personally and professionally. That gave me an inner peace that is so worth having. On top of that, it gives you confidence and self-esteem that no one in the world can knock down.

Why did I decide to write this book?

My journey in science was an interesting one it has taught me many lessons; so, I wanted to share the human side of it. I did not see any scientists share the personal side of their journey and the challenges that they faced. I wanted to share my story that nothing is impossible to achieve.

Personally, as a scientist, I believe that I hold a responsibility toward the next generation by helping them and guiding them to the correct career pathway. Mentoring them to reach their potential not just in science.

They are surrounded by so many options thanks to the technology, I think it can be overwhelming sometimes which can be a two-edged sword, it will make you think that you know what you want, and you may feel lost at times.

We live a fast-paced life we are getting impatient; we forgot that reaching our goals requires time, effort, and patients you cannot cut corners to reach your goals or achieve success in life. To approach your long-term goals, you need to be aware that it is a process, from my experience it will shape you both personally and professionally.

I am not telling you don't aim high but be realistic when setting up your goals and at the same time be aware that this is a journey, let me give you an example, compare yourself when you did your degree to the time that you started, you were not the same person there was growth right! Think how far you have changed since then.

Let me simplify it for you think how far you have changed 3 or 6 months ago and reflect on how much you have changed since then.

I want to share with you the thoughts that I went through, I want to give you hope that no dream is impossible to achieve. If you are feeling down and you need motivation, I am your friend, this book will remind you that you can do whatever you want, all you need is to believe in yourself and go and get what you deserve.

This journey taught me that if I want to grow these should be my best friend's commitment, perseverance, dedication and on top of that not giving up on my goals.

I am a strong believer that we rise by lifting each other, so everything that I am sharing with you here is from experience. I am aware that every journey is different, and to be honest, I do not want you to make the same mistakes that I have made.

I hope that this will help you when you feel like you are about to give up on your dream, please don't because I can assure you the feeling of accomplishing that goal is so rewarding, you will forget the hard times, I love that saying the harder it is the sweeter the victory.

I will be sharing with you some of the lessons that in my opinion are valuable, they are all based on my own experience no matter what walk of life you are in.

I defined my goal.

This is the most important part of my journey, I needed to remind myself at every stage of my journey.

What are my goals, why are so important to me, how can achieve my goals and how can they help me to achieve my dream of becoming a qualified scientist?

This also taught me that having a vision was particularly important, I was visualising where I wanted to be, I wanted to become a qualified scientist. How I will feel being there. How I will feel when I make my dream come true.

Knowing your goal is crucial because that will give you the strength and the patience to keep going when you face difficulties.

The starting point was when I was calling different hospitals, I had to be precise and straight to the point to ask if they can help me to work and if they can offer me the help to train. I treated it as if it is my right to ask for a chance to grow and progress.

In my case, I had to remind myself that no matter what happens and no matter how long I will get qualified and make my dream come true. I also reminded myself that I did not study and work so hard to give up now, I will fight for this, and I must keep going.

After many rejections, I finally got a yes and a maybe. One said maybe? send us an email and we will get back to you, the other one said yes send me an email.

I did email them both, I said to myself I will follow and go with the one that replies first which I did. I was so happy I could have given up after many rejections, but I was determined, that it was a one-way road for me.

I had to make my proposal very clear, I remember I emailed the manager why I wanted to work there, and my goal was to qualify while working there. So, I was being specific when I addressed my goal and stood by it, I never knew that I would get challenged at times, I stood my ground as I might get asked why I want it or in other words, do I want it?

This helped me to know why and what I wanted to achieve, I wanted to get qualified.

I had to remind myself I chose this career because I want to make a difference in healthcare through my service.

This has indeed helped me overcome the challenges and the adversities because as you get closer to your goal it gets harder. It is like you are being told "Do you want it or how bad do you want it?". I learned when I am in this stage of any challenge, I should remind myself why I started so that can keep going.

Planning is also important, to keep reviewing my plan and goals. I remember because I was not a trainee, for my training process to keep moving forward it was depending on many factors to get my training going. For example, the availability of the resources, the time to train, the availability of training officers etc. I had to keep track of the process and keep pushing if my goals were getting compromised. Like any project, you need to plan well.

Here I have learned that I love planning, organising, executing, and presenting my work. I developed this skill more when I did my Master's and when I worked in a pharmaceutical company as a research scientist, it became natural to me to organise projects including this book that you are reading now. I discovered that it is a natural talent that I have.

This has made me discover that I have this skill naturally in me, which I see as a blessing.

I learnt that life is more than just studying, graduating, and spending the rest of your life working until you retire.

I eliminated the fear of failure.

This in my opinion is the main obstacle that most of us face in life, which stops us from living the life that we want. This was one of the main reasons that I believe stopped me from taking that risky step, of leaving my current position when I was not going anywhere, and I needed to try somewhere else and start again.

The first thing that comes into your mind, when you are facing any challenge or anything new is I cannot do it, or I do not know. So, you limit yourself without even trying or giving yourself the chance to even try!

When I moved to London to start my university life after graduating from high school in the UAE. I had an amazing time; I was a hardworking student disciplined with great schoolwork ethics etc. This has made the transition phase easier than I thought. I was always fascinated by science, and I enjoyed school, so I chose science as a career.

At university, I developed, and I felt adjusted to the UK, then I graduated it was all good so far.

The only problem that I could not overcome was the fear of failure, it took me a very long time to figure out where this fear originated from, we were raised at school that if you get good grades and do well you will do well in life. So, we were always aiming to get top grades and attached our happiness and peace of mind to that. I am not blaming anyone here I am trying to explain how this feeling grew in me.

I do not know why I was worried; I had no reason to I wish that I learned that if you do your best, you will get top grades because that is what used to happen, I study well I get good grades. I was not at the top of my class, but I had the most important skill of all I work smart.

I guess it was peer pressure we used to compare with each other, so we needed to build a reputation on who got the best and who is the first etc I am sure you can all relate to that.

Unfortunately, that did not change when I was at university, in a different country UK. I had a new challenge here in London the language, I was studying Arabic back in UAE, but I overcome that quickly and then I graduated.

I loved moving to the UK experiencing a different educational culture has its benefits and you develop an amazing skill that helps your professional development.

I still carried the feeling of fearing failure with me, the positive side of that is that pushed me to do my best.

Even when I completed my bachelor's degree, I could not challenge myself to push boundaries and the fear of failure changed I had another companion, the fear of rejection as I started to apply for jobs, and I was not successful.

This has changed following MSc it was a wonderful experience I got my first research position as a Research Scientist in an area where I did my research, I was over the moon.

The biggest test was when I decided to branch out and enter the clinical and the medical field, little that I know it was a hell of a journey filled with personal and professional transformation. Here was the biggest challenge of all.

I stopped waiting for the right moment.

Waiting for the perfect moment was my worst enemy and overplanning was caused by the fear of failure. I was afraid of the unknown, the change. So, I kept waiting for the perfect conditions i.e., looking for a trainee position, rather than looking for other options. There were other options such as working as assistance with different conditions part-time or as bank staff or agency staff etc.

I remember I was scared to begin the journey of taking the steps to qualify to find a trainee position and going back to university to top up modules, which was a common problem in my profession little that I knew that it is doable, and it requires dedication, patience, and persistence. So, I did my top-up modules, I self-funded my courses and still no ray of hope to get training in the laboratory in my current position.

Here I had to decide to take a new step and find a way to make my goal to qualify as a Biomedical Scientist, I remember I called every hospital in London and had no success. Then a random search I cannot remember how but I believe God has guided me to this, I found two hospitals outside London and managed to negotiate something. I decided to go to the one that responded quicker.

Because I knew my goal, I was honest I explained to the laboratory manager my situation and I wanted to work for the department and in return, I get the support to get trained get qualified, this was my first ever career-negotiation experience. When I analysed this, I realised that negotiation can be applied everywhere. It is a win-win situation. You work for me, and I offer you the training and the support to qualify.

I remember that time when I decided to start all over again, I was terrified, but this was a whole new journey that consisted of not just professional transformation but also personal growth.

Here I learned that once you have a vision and a sketch of your plan then you take the first step, things do work out by themselves, and more ideas appear out of nowhere. Just like magic. I see that as a reward.

I got offered a bank position, and a temporary position as an assistant and thankfully I got a permeant one within two months. I see that is a blessing to any change just take the first step and the rest will follow.

I now embrace change and I welcome it because I believe that every change brings a better you and it will bring more and better opportunities that will take you to better places.

I also learned that I should always ask and never fear getting a no answer, eventually, I will get a yes even if I got a nine NOs the tenth one will be a YES!

Adaptability and flexibility, they became my best friends.

Another valuable lesson that I had to learn, and I still practice it up to this day.

Adaptability is about the powerful difference between adapting to cope and adapting to win." Max McKeown, Adaptability: The Art of Winning in an Age of Uncertainty

Believing in your dream and goals is the first thing you do before you approach any goal, as this will be the driving force for you towards achieving your goals.

I had to start all over again in a new place outside London, with a longer commute, in a new place and a new environment. I did not realise that life is a journey that consists of a series of journeys anyway. This was the best experience ever I enjoyed it. I learned more about the laboratory setting in the National Health Services (NHS) I had an overall experience. This has enhanced my career immensely.

So, I had to learn that I have to accept the fact that I will encounter changes and adapt to them. Some of those changes would make me uncomfortable. I used to hate feeling uncomfortable or not knowing what to do next if I can avoid I would.

I think the problem was that I would always think of the things that would go wrong, so I changed the way that I see change and think of the things that could go right, this has helped me to welcome any change or challenge that would make me better. I have learned that having a positive mindset can make all the difference.

So, I learned to go with the flow and adapted to any change I started to get excited by it, still, sometimes I do struggle but with practice, it works every time. They say change is the only constant. Think about it, we have day and night, sunrise, and sunset. This happens every single day.

So, when approaching a challenge, now I welcome it and embrace it because of my strong belief that it will bring more opportunities with it.

I believe nowadays we need to be adaptable and flexible. The world is changing at an unprecedented pace. You need an open mind combined with flexibility and adaptability; I think this will keep you at ease in my opinion. This will help you be comfortable with the rapid changes that we are facing all the time

Patience also became my best friend.

In this day and age, we all lack patience, particularly since everything is instant. In my journey I had to learn to be patient and that this will be a process. I had to appreciate that I have a different path than my peers, and I had to accept that my path will be different.

When I decided to leap, I had to learn to adjust and remind myself that we are all humans, and we all have the same brain and willpower.

I will never be limited by how long it will take me or how much it will cost me, I always thought of the ultimate goal, I want to become a qualified scientist.

I learned that we have a choice, this is what I told myself and trained myself to encourage myself to continue to progress. We are humans we have the brain, the ability and determination compared to other creatures. When we want something, we can have it, we do not just exist for survival- eat, sleep and repeat.

I had to learn that there is no easy life, there is life with purpose, aims and goals. When I realised that fact life became so much easier.

Looking back, I am so grateful that I did not give up and I learned that everything happens for a reason. As I am writing these words it is all making sense to me why I took this route and what I have learned from it that I am sharing with you now.

So, when you are on a journey, be patient it takes time never think of taking shortcuts.

There is nothing wrong with being different.

I had to learn that there is nothing wrong with taking a different path. When I thought deeply about this, I realised I always hated to follow the majority, then I realised that being different is a gift.

When I started my journey, I learned more about myself and noticed signs through my journey, and I made sure that I was aware of them at every step of my journey.

I have learned that everything happens for a reason, and I had to pay attention to those signs. I remember watching a talk where Steven Spielberg American film director, producer, and screenwriter said "Sometimes a dream almost whispers... it never shouts. Very hard to hear. So, you have to, every day of your lives, be ready to hear what whispers in your ear."

I believe we do not grow physically we grow personally and mentally; all you need is to stay calm and focused on your goal. That can be challenging at times, but I have learned that with practice. I have not mastered it because pressure can come in different shapes and forms, but I believe since the feeling is the same, therefore the protective steps are the same.

I needed to be prepared for it once I see the signs, anytime I felt weak I would remind myself that this situation is temporary, and it will pass. Because if I do not the feeling of regret will last for a lifetime, and I will never forgive myself for that.

Mastering the art of limiting distractions.

I believe limiting distractions it is an art. Currently, this has become an essential skill that we need more than ever, as we are surrounded by many distractions, which make it exceedingly difficult for all of us to achieve our goals.

I too do lose my focus I am a human being after all, but the way I get myself out of it is by treating my goals as if like I am in an exam. Think how we are when we are sitting an exam and under exam conditions. Even when I am writing this book, I am treating it as an exam.

What I have learned that, that this is the life we have to get used to organising our priorities and getting them done accordingly.

I came across a great method for achieving my goals it is called the SMART approach the SMART acronym stands for Specific, Measurable, Achievable, Realistic, and Timely. It is a tool that you can use to plan and achieve your goals it can also be used guide in the setting of goals and objectives for better results

I will leave you to do your research about that, but it is useful and worth applying. So, you can avoid setting big and unrealistic goals which we all tend to do.

I did stay focused and made sure that I dedicated my time to my aim, I still enjoyed myself and allowed time for breaks etc. However, I was in a "now or never" mode. Limiting distractions is a skill, like any skill you acquire it takes time to build. So, it is very important to have the ability to focus and do your best.

I became aware of my routine and my habits.

I always had a routine, but I never paid attention to it as I was naturally organised since I was at school. I was always strict with myself I prioritised my studies, in the UAE we were brought up like that. I was glad, to be honest as I saw the difference when I moved to the UK as there is more freedom and more distractions.

However, when I started working that became challenging to achieve. So, I developed a sense of understanding of my habits. I learned that in the last five years after years of exploring.

Here I was stricter with myself, I started from scratch. I observed my sleeping times, and my daily routine. So, I started applying those small changes, such as going to bed early and waking up earlier not the typical 6 am. I used to wake up super early if I had a deadline or a mission to accomplish.

So, I decided to join the 5 am club, then slowly that got earlier to sometimes 3 or even 2 am, in extreme cases depending on what work that I planned to do.

The morning routine was the turning point for me, although since my school days I used to study or revise at 3 or 4 am I did not think of it as a habit when I became a professional.

But I tell you this is so worth it, you might have heard this before, but from my personal experience I call the 4 am club the "Elite Club". Naturally, we would wake up for morning prayer "Fajr" there are many benefits to that, so you can apply that in your modern or normal lives.

You will be surprised how much you can do in the 2 or 3 hours or even 1 hr. Start small for 1 hour then increase it. The results are magical you have already started your day before everybody else and you have already ticked some of your tasks.

Another morning habit that I have developed was going to the gym and exercising, you do not need me to say how beneficial that can be. I used to work out after my working day. Once I swapped it with exercising before work, yes sometimes challenging but personally, it has changed my life around. Think of it you will wake up to start your day whether you like it or not, so you might as well wake up and do what you want.

Try it for yourself!

Building healthy habits take time, I sometimes like everyone else I do get side tracked. But I go back and carry on which leads me to the next point.

Get used to restating when you go off track. This is another habit that you need to master in my opinion because nowadays can get distracted at an unknown rate it can be exceedingly difficult to stay focused.

Building healthy habits, in general, can be hard at first like anything in life, they do take time to build, and they require patience and determination as you build them small. But I guarantee you the long-term benefits are priceless.

I took calculated risks.

After years of working for the same company and department with no progression, I had to decide to start all over again. That was the hardest decision that I had to make but at the same time, this was a blessing. Any change or challenge always leads to an opportunity when approached correctly.

It requires you to be true to yourself and face the challenge. At that particular time, I realised that I did not push myself far enough and I did not take that brave step of weighing my options and going through the process of growth.

This was my first experience of taking a route to better myself alone. This experience of training while working is not new. but no one tells you that you need to fight the fight. The lessons gained here were valuable, as they have helped me in the following transitional journeys.

This gave me an experience on how to accept new challenges in my career and my life in general. It got bigger and bigger; I shall share more in my next publications.

The skill of negotiation.

During my registration journey as I was training voluntarily while working as an assistant, I had to learn to negotiate almost every step that I needed to take to reach my goal of qualifying

Everything is negotiable regardless of where you are. This is what I have learned always ask what is the worse that could happen. You never know where this can take you.

I had to learn to be sensible while negotiating, it was hard at the beginning but with practice, this became a skill that led to becoming a natural talent. I learned this involved me knowing myself and my environment, and not blaming others for any shortcomings. It is my responsibility to push for my dream to come true regardless of the opposition.

For example, sometimes laboratories can be remarkably busy, and I am trying to get my work marked or I require signatures all that can be delayed here I had to negotiate if I can get the time where I can an answer or if I needed attention. Having the skill of negotiating and being diplomatic can help you when used appropriately.

Professional mentorship.

I was not lucky enough to have a career mentor or a professional mentor. There was a career service at the university, but that was not very popular at my time we were overwhelmed as it is with our studies and the never-ending course deadlines. Also, I think the job market was not as saturated as it is these days, or so I thought.

I remember I got an email from the university inviting me to participate in professional mentoring. I remember I wanted to help other students in their career journey particularly in science I did not want anyone to go through what I have gone through to get qualified. I signed up and it has been years since then, I still participate in this programme up to this day.

Since the first time that I have taken part in professional mentoring years ago, it has inspired me to have my professional career coach and a professional mentor, I cannot recommend it enough that having a professional coach and a mentor can make a massive difference in your career journey.

Why do I still participate in professional mentoring? I believe that it is my duty as a professional to reach back to the next generation and help them as Don't just aspire to make a living, aspire to make a difference." — Denzel Washington.

I also enjoy taking part in this amazing programme, because I enjoy sharing what I have learned from my career journey, I did not have a career coach when I was a student, so I struggled in my career, so I do not want any other student to go through what I went through.

I love mentoring university students to help them before they enter the professional field or workforce. My advice to you all university students, make sure that you enrol on the Mentoring Schemes do not just focus on your studies, you need to learn more about your career path and skills before you graduate. The University gives you so many opportunities to look out for them and make use of them.

Keep looking for the next goal.

As I am writing these words as I have completed one goal. I am working towards one and already thinking of my next goal. I learned to keep learning, to keep growing and to keep challenging myself.

As we grow in age, we should continue to grow with bigger ambitions and aspirations. The world will continue to evolve and so should we.

You might be thinking this is another self-help book. The reason I wanted to share my story, is I wanted to share the personal side of trying to become a qualified healthcare scientist, the skills that I have gained have helped me to become the person that I wanted to become. I saw how these challenges could lead you to more opportunities which I will share more in my next publications.

I hope to inspire as many people as possible out there and make you believe that anything is possible to achieve when you believe that you can do it. You need to have the faith in God and your abilities, determination, dedication, and patience. I remind myself little progression is better than no progression.

Never give up.

This story is where I have learned this, even when looked impossible to reach my goal.

As you get closer to your goal it can get incredibly challenging. Little that I knew it was the toughest one for me, it was so tough that I almost gave up, but I am sharing it so that you too know that you should never give up.

I was at the final stages to submit my application to get my assessment for verification to become Biomedical Scientist. As I was getting all the paperwork ready with my training officer, I realised that the period for me to apply had expired. Oh my God, this was the worst feeling I would not wish on my worst enemy.

I was at my lowest, I remember I got in touch with the organisation responsible on the phone and they said that I will have to get re-assessed and potentially I might have to pay for an additional top-up module, which I have to study and pass before I re-apply for my application to be assessed. Yes, I have to go back to university to study.

I was on the phone with the admin personnel, I cried, and I said I am not going to this anymore I cannot this is getting too long. The lady was so sympathetic, and she said "No you have gone so far, don't give up now as you are so close to getting qualified"

I am so grateful for this lady as she made a difference for me not to give up now, after all these years and the hard work.

So, I got re-assessed my application and sadly I had to do another top-up module. I give in and I spent the whole weekend crying and feeling sorry for myself, worst of all at work I had to face everyone on Monday and explain what has happened. But I kept my head up and prayed to God to give me the strength to keep going. I did I finished the module and I passed with flying colours within 8 weeks,

I discovered sometimes setbacks can make us discover how strong we can be. Two months later I got qualified, and the feedback was amazing too. I was on top of the world I went to the moon and back it was so worth it.

Taking the longer way does not mean failure.

Taking the longer route in pursuing my first career journey in science and the challenges that I faced, have taught me many lessons. I truly believe that those lessons can apply to anyone who is about to start their career or business.

Once you know yourself and your goals you will know what you want, it is quite simple, yet it requires time and for you to be adaptable, comfortable with changes and the challenges that you will face, and on top of all never giving up on dreams and goals. It is a process that requires patience and faith.

Final thoughts.

I believe that career challenges are the same and the lessons that are learned are crucial. You need to be aware of them to be able to make the right decision when you are at a crossroads situation.

Whether you are a student or someone who is about to start work or even a business. The challenges are the same regardless of what career path you take, but if you learn those lessons, it will help you reach your goals, and it will help you to keep aiming high. I would not have learned those lessons if I took the standard or the straightforward way.

Taking the harder way does not make you a failure. No, you learn more about yourself and you will benefit from it, as this will shape not just professionally but also personally.

I discovered that knowing myself is the key to all successes. Once you know who you are, you will know what you want and where you want to be.

I hope that my journey will give hope to you all, not to give up on your dreams no matter how difficult this can be you can make it happen.

Whatever happens, remember nothing is impossible to achieve, you simply have to put in the work and belief in God, yourself, and your abilities. Then you will become unstoppable. Never stop dreaming. Keep shining and inspiring.

Printed in Great Britain
by Amazon